FROM THE FILMS OF

Harry Potter™

FRIENDS AND FOES

A MOVIE SCRAPBOOK

WIZARDING WORLD

INSIGHT EDITIONS

SAN RAFAEL · LOS ANGELES · LONDON

CONTENTS

After eleven-year-old Harry Potter learns he's a wizard, it's an easy choice for him to decide between staying with cruel, intolerant relatives or following a half giant to a magical community that offers him acceptance and support. To his surprise, Harry is already well-known in the wizarding world. When Harry was an infant, Lord Voldemort marked him as the only one who could stop the Dark wizard's desire for unconditional rule. This is not a task Harry can accomplish alone, however, although he often tries. In order to defeat Voldemort and his Death Eaters, the friendships Harry makes during his journey will be as important as his magical skills to his success.

Harry Potter, played by Daniel Radcliffe in the eight-part film series, meets his two best friends while traveling to school: Ron Weasley, played by Rupert Grint, who comes from a large and loving ginger-haired family, and Hermione Granger, a smart, resourceful witch played by Emma Watson. "Harry, Ron, and Hermione really are a unit," says Radcliffe. "As you watch the films, you feel that Harry's strong as long as he's got them by his side."

Harry also forms steadfast friendships with fellow students, Ron's siblings and parents, and sympathetic professors. Their wisdom and encouragement influence Harry as he pursues his daunting task. Harry influences those around him as well—through their friendship, for example, Neville Longbottom gains so much faith in himself, he ends up leading the resistance against Voldemort.

However, not everyone at Hogwarts is so friendly to Harry. Draco Malfoy consistently bullies him during their school years. Draco's family is part of Voldemort's inner circle, who work against Harry and his friends whenever possible. Harry also finds himself the target of several teachers' wrath, most notably Potions professor Severus Snape. Snape is antagonistic and hostile to Harry, though Harry cannot understand why.

Like most people, Harry might not know initially who is a friend and who is a foe. Dobby the house-elf tries to prevent Harry from staying at Hogwarts in *Harry Potter and the Chamber of Secrets*, with actions that often prove catastrophic. But Dobby's motivation is heartfelt—he knows that his master is plotting against Harry. Sirius Black, Harry's godfather, is rumored to have betrayed Harry's parents—but when the truth is revealed, Sirius proves a loving mentor. Professor Alastor Moody is a foe in *Harry Potter and the Goblet of Fire* when a Polyjuice-Potioned Death Eater replaces him, but later he's a friend as a member of the Order of the Phoenix, sworn to protect Harry and defeat Voldemort.

Occasionally, foes can actually become friends. As a child, Draco Malfoy was bullied by his father, but when that influence lessens, Draco chooses to save Harry when he is captured by Draco's aunt and parents. The most surprising revelation to Harry is that, for his own reasons, the smug, unyielding Severus Snape has actually been in his corner all along.

As Sirius Black tells Harry, "We've all got both light and dark inside us. What matters is the part we choose to act on. That's who we really are."

RON WEASLEY

Harry Potter and Ron Weasley become friends on the Hogwarts Express as they head to their first year at Hogwarts School of Witchcraft and Wizardry. Ron's impressed by Harry's lightning-bolt scar, and even more impressed when Harry purchases a whole lot of sweets. Their friendship lasts a lifetime.

> ## "I'M RON, BY THE WAY. RON WEASLEY."
>
> *Ron Weasley, Harry Potter and the Sorcerer's Stone*

HAVING A LAUGH

Harry and Ron have a believable friendship as the actors playing them bonded before filming. Sometimes, however, a real-life friendship can work against actors. While filming in the Hogwarts Express carriage, the boys struggled to complete a take. "We were constantly giggling," remembers Rupert Grint. "We couldn't film it together, so we had to do it separately. [Director] Chris Columbus would play Harry's part when they were filming me, and then he would play me with Dan."

Ron's confidence sinks to a new low before his first Quidditch match, so Harry pretends to pour Felix Felicis—Liquid Luck— into his breakfast juice. Now believing that luck is on his side, Ron excels as Keeper, and Gryffindor wins the game.

BOYS!

Ron's jealousy gets the better of him when Harry becomes a champion for the Triwizard Tournament in *Harry Potter and the Goblet of Fire*. "I think because Harry's always the hero and an amazing Quidditch player and he's always saving the school, Ron does get a bit angry and annoyed," says Rupert Grint. After Ron witnesses the danger of the first task, he offers something resembling an apology. "They come to arguments at the beginning, but they're still good friends," Grint confirms.

HE'S A KEEPER

Ron achieves his dream of making the Quidditch team in *Harry Potter and the Half-Blood Prince* with a little help from his friends. At tryouts, Ron doesn't appear to have much talent at the game. This was achieved by having the crew set up challenges for Grint, such as throwing twenty Quaffles at him. To secure the role of Keeper for Ron, Hermione secretly casts the Confundus Charm at his competition, Cormac McLaggen, who misses a crucial Quaffle.

HERMIONE GRANGER

Harry and Ron form a deep friendship with Hermione Granger, though they're both initially put off by her know-it-all attitude, aversion to rule-breaking, and fear of imperfection. These qualities are mitigated by Hermione's intelligence and loyalty, however, both of which save their skins myriad times.

> "ME? BOOKS AND CLEVERNESS. THERE ARE MORE IMPORTANT THINGS. FRIENDSHIP AND BRAVERY."
>
> Hermione Granger, *Harry Potter and the Sorcerer's Stone*

Hermione takes the blame for trying to defeat a troll in *Harry Potter and the Sorcerer's Stone* so Harry and Ron don't get into trouble.

SCARED STIFF

Once Hermione is cured from Petrification in *Harry Potter and the Chamber of Secrets*, she reunites with Harry and Ron in the Great Hall. "I remember being so angry at [director] Chris Columbus because I had to hug Dan," says Watson. "How could he make me throw my arms around a boy in front of everyone?" Watson hugged Radcliffe quickly, then let go. For the hug to appear worthwhile, Columbus freeze-framed the shot to extend the moment. The director got back on Watson's good side by allowing her to only shake hands with Grint.

> **"ONE OF MY BEST FRIENDS IS MUGGLE-BORN. SHE'S THE BEST IN OUR YEAR."**
>
> Harry Potter, *Harry Potter and the Half-Blood Prince*

GOOD FAITH

Harry initially resists when Hermione asks him to teach defensive spells to their fellow students in *Harry Potter and the Order of the Phoenix*. "Hermione convinces him, because she really believes he has something to give people," says Watson. "I think one of the really touching elements to Hermione and Harry's story is that even when he doesn't have faith in himself, she does. And that's what friends are for."

CARE TO DANCE ✦✦✦✦✦✦✦✦✦✦✦✦✦

Harry and Ron have an argument while searching for Horcruxes in *Harry Potter and the Deathly Hallows – Part 1*, and Ron Apparates away, leaving Hermione distraught. Usually, it's Hermione supporting Harry. In an effort to console her, Harry coaxes her into dancing with him. "I don't think there are very many friendships like Hermione and Harry's in literature or onscreen," Watson says. "I love moments where you see and understand their friendship, and they're few and far between."

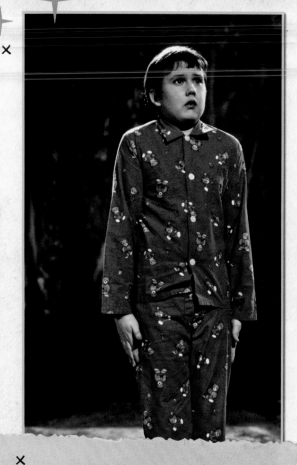

The magical skills of fellow Gryffindor Neville Longbottom, played by Matthew Lewis, might be in doubt, but the loyalty to his house and his classmates is not. When he catches Hermione, Harry, and Ron sneaking out of the common room at night in *Harry Potter and the Sorcerer's Stone*, he tries to prevent them from leaving, but Neville doesn't stand a chance. With great regret, Hermione casts *Petrificus Totalus* on him.

"IT TAKES A GREAT DEAL OF BRAVERY TO STAND UP TO YOUR ENEMIES, BUT A GREAT DEAL MORE TO STAND UP TO YOUR FRIENDS. I AWARD TEN POINTS TO NEVILLE LONGBOTTOM."

Professor Albus Dumbledore,
Harry Potter and the Sorcerer's Stone

In their first flying lesson, Harry sticks up for Neville when Draco Malfoy steals Neville's Remembrall, making Neville indirectly responsible for Harry becoming the youngest Seeker in a century on the Gryffindor Quidditch team.

SEEKER

IN THE WEEDS

Neville's typically despairing mindset changes in *Harry Potter and the Goblet of Fire* when he helps Harry with the Triwizard Tournament's second task, suggesting gillyweed so Harry can swim underwater for an hour. Harry chokes a bit on the herb and falls into the water, leaving Neville fearful he's killed him. "But when Harry brings up Ron and Fleur's sister from the lake, Neville's mood completely changes," says Lewis. "He's extremely happy because he knows he's helped his friend."

IN CONFIDENCE

Lewis believes that as Harry looked out for Neville, as he gained confidence, he was inspired to do the same for his classmates. "He really comes into his own," says Lewis. "He changes beyond anyone's expectations, becoming a great leader and a great man."

Luna Lovegood

Luna Lovegood, played by Evanna Lynch, is decidedly unique, but as Harry comes to know her, she is truly kind and a great comfort to him. Surprisingly logical, her voice may be soft, but her loyalty to Harry and his mission is solid.

Luna's a Ravenclaw but supports her friends even when they're not in her house. For Ron's first Quidditch match in *Harry Potter and the Half-Blood Prince*, Luna wears a lion hat as a tribute to the Gryffindors. Evanna Lynch suggested that it appear as if the lion is eating her head.

AT THE OUTSIDE

Lynch feels that Luna and Harry have a special bond, from both being outsiders. "He wants to fit in with everyone," she explains, "but everyone's against him because of what happened with Voldemort." Luna is an outsider as "everyone sees her as different and a bit odd." Lynch believes Harry is fascinated by her "because she speaks the truth. She's so honest all the time."

TAKE ON TRUST

Harry comes upon Luna feeding Thestrals in the forest in *Harry Potter and the Order of the Phoenix*, where he expresses doubt anyone believes he fought Voldemort. Luna disagrees and offers an insight that encourages him to count on his friends: "Well, if I were You-Know-Who, I'd want you to feel cut off from everyone else. Because if it's just you alone, you're not as much of a threat."

DRESSING THE PART

During the holidays, Harry attends Professor Horace Slughorn's party, where he wants to bring a friend. When he finds Hermione unavailable, he invites Luna, who wears a dress that resembles a Christmas tree. "I doubt she goes to many of these kinds of things," says Lynch, "so she's using this opportunity to dress up, as she imagines it, properly."

In *Harry Potter and the Deathly Hallows - Part 2*, Luna tells Harry to talk to the ghost of Helena Ravenclaw in order to find the Ravenclaw Diadem Horcrux. "There's not a person alive who's seen it," she tells him. "It's obvious, isn't it? We have to talk to someone who's dead."

GINNY WEASLEY

Ginny Weasley is the youngest of seven Weasley siblings and the only girl. After meeting Harry Potter at Platform Nine and Three-Quarters in *Harry Potter and the Sorcerer's Stone*, Ginny develops a crush on him, but it takes quite a while before Harry realizes how much she means to him.

FIRST LOVE

"Obviously she's in awe of him," says Bonnie Wright, who plays Ginny Weasley. "In *Harry Potter and the Chamber of Secrets*, she runs away at the sight of him!" Wright assumed that as Harry was so close to the Weasleys, they would develop a sibling-like relationship. "I was honestly quite oblivious to the fact that they would eventually end up together."

UNCOMMON BONDS

In *Harry Potter and the Chamber of Secrets*, Ginny is unknowingly possessed by Tom Riddle's diary, which causes her to release the Basilisk, a murderous serpent, into Hogwarts. Then Ginny is forced to enter the Chamber herself, where Harry saves her. "This makes her realize the danger that he's in," Wright explains, "and what it's like to be completely taken over by Lord Voldemort." When Harry is controlled by Voldemort in *Harry Potter and the Order of the Phoenix*, "her experience [gives] Ginny an insight into Harry no one else could have."

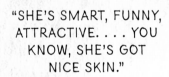

"SHE'S SMART, FUNNY, ATTRACTIVE. . . . YOU KNOW, SHE'S GOT NICE SKIN."

Harry Potter, *Harry Potter and the Half-Blood Prince*

TAKING CHARGE ✦✦✦✦✦✦✦✦✦✦✦✦✦✦✦

Ginny notices a parallel between Harry's obsession with the Half-Blood Prince's Potions book, in *Harry Potter and the Half-Blood Prince*, and her being manipulated by Tom Riddle's diary. Insisting he hide the book, she takes him to the Room of Requirement to conceal it, then steals a kiss from Harry. Both Bonnie Wright and Daniel Radcliffe described filming the kiss as "weird." "It was a bit awkward at first," adds Wright, but she liked that "Ginny had the confidence to initiate the first physical anything" between her and Harry.

GRYFFINDORS

FRED AND GEORGE WEASLEY

Fred and George Weasley, Ron's older twin brothers played by James and Oliver Phelps, present Harry with the Marauder's Map—which allows the user to see where everyone is in Hogwarts at any given time—in *Harry Potter and the Prisoner of Azkaban*. Could there be any better act of friendship?

ALL OVER THE MAP

Fred and George spot Harry using his Invisibility Cloak to get to Hogsmeade and pull him inside from the snow to give him the Marauder's Map, a scene that will always stand out for Oliver Phelps. "It was the first time that Fred and George became a big influence on what goes on," he explains. Another reason it will stand out? "It was shot on the hottest day of the year," Oliver remembers. "And we with our woolly coats on. We had to stop a few times because we were sweating so much!"

"WHAT'S THIS RUBBISH, HE SAYS?"

"THAT THERE IS THE SECRET TO OUR SUCCESS. IT'S A WRENCH GIVING IT TO YOU, BELIEVE ME, BUT WE'VE DECIDED, YOUR NEEDS ARE GREATER THAN OURS."

Fred and George Weasley,
Harry Potter and the Prisoner of Azkaban

SEAMUS FINNIGAN AND DEAN THOMAS

Seamus Finnigan and Dean Thomas, played by Devon Murray and Alfred Enoch, round out Harry's Gryffindor dormmates. Seamus and Dean are a pair as close as Harry and Ron.

CONFLICT OF INTEREST

In *Harry Potter and the Order of the Phoenix*, "Seamus's mom has been telling him not to believe anything Harry's saying about Voldemort," says Murray. This puts Seamus and Dean into conflict. "Dean believes Harry, but, of course, he's best friends with Seamus," says Enoch. When Seamus learns Death Eaters have escaped Azkaban, "He comes round," Enoch continues, "and realizes this is a serious situation."

DUMBLEDORE'S ARMY

When their Defense Against the Dark Arts professor, Dolores Umbridge, won't teach defensive spells in *Harry Potter and the Order of the Phoenix*, Hermione persuades Harry to become instructor to a group of interested students, who call themselves Dumbledore's Army.

"At first, Harry's a really reluctant teacher," says Radcliffe. "He's talked into it by Hermione, and as usual, she's irritating and right."

"MAYBE YOU DON'T HAVE TO DO THIS ALL BY YOURSELF, MATE."

Ron Weasley, *Harry Potter and the Order of the Phoenix*

CONFIDENCE BUILDING

Neville eagerly joins Dumbledore's Army, though he considers himself hopeless. Harry's faith in him does a lot to bolster his confidence and his wand skills. In *Harry Potter and the Deathly Hallows – Part 2*, Neville takes charge of an ad hoc Dumbledore's Army. "Neville assumes the responsibility of the leader of this rebellion," says Matthew Lewis. "That's due a lot to Harry."

As a tribute to Harry's favorite teacher, Daniel Radcliffe asked director David Yates if he could wear an outfit that could evoke the humble appearance of Professor Remus Lupin.

GREAT EXPECTATIONS

One of the most exciting spells Harry teaches Dumbledore's Army is *Expecto Patronum*, which casts a Patronus—a positive force that takes the form of a shield or an animal—used to deflect Dementors. Luna Lovegood's Patronus is a hare, but when it came time to perform the spell, "I was a bit disappointed," says Lynch. "I said *Expecto Patronum* and not a thing came out of my wand, you know!"

REBELS WITH A CAUSE

Fred and George Weasley trust Harry, says Oliver Phelps, "and they want to help him." There's another, more Fred-and-George-type reason that both Oliver and James believe they join Dumbledore's Army. "It's not only because it's got to be done," says James Phelps, "but also because it's a way for them to stick it to what Umbridge's done to the school."

Hogwarts is joined by two European wizarding schools for the Triwizard Tournament in *Harry Potter and the Goblet of Fire*. The point of the tournament is not fame or glory but, as Hermione says, "to make friends."

> "IN LIGHT OF RECENT EVENTS, THE BONDS OF FRIENDSHIP WE MADE THIS YEAR WILL BE MORE IMPORTANT THAN EVER."
>
> Professor Albus Dumbledore,
> *Harry Potter and the Goblet of Fire*

✦ CEDRIC DIGGORY →

Cedric Diggory, played by Robert Pattinson, is the Hogwarts Champion. "He's competitive," says Pattinson, "but gets his priorities right in the end." Harry informs Cedric about the first task; Cedric reciprocates for the second. After Cedric's death, Dumbledore describes him as a "fierce, fierce friend."

FLEUR DELACOUR

Fleur Delacour, the Beauxbatons Champion, is "eternally grateful to Harry," says actress Clémence Poésy. "Fleur is attacked by Grindylows during the second task and cannot rescue her sister, Gabrielle." When Harry realizes she has withdrawn, he saves both Ron and Gabrielle.

+·+·+·+·+·+·+·+·+·+·+·+·+

VIKTOR KRUM

Durmstrang Champion Viktor Krum is, as actor Stanislav Ianevski describes him, "a nice guy but more of a physical being than a talkative one." Krum invites Hermione Granger to the Yule Ball, where a jealous Ron grumbles, "I think he's got a bit more than friendship on his mind."

HOGWARTS PROFESSORS

Albus Dumbledore

Albus Dumbledore, Hogwarts Headmaster, evolves from a protector of Harry Potter to a mentor and friend. Dumbledore orchestrates Harry's rescue after his parents are killed and does all he can to help Harry defeat Voldemort.

FIRST OF ALL

Actor Richard Harris "was always the first choice for Dumbledore," says director Chris Columbus. "We needed a father figure," adds producer David Heyman, "who, at the same time, had a twinkle in his eye—someone who had a sense of mischief." Sadly, Harris died after the second film, *Harry Potter and the Chamber of Secrets*, and the part was recast with Michael Gambon.

> "YOU SHOULD KNOW . . . PROFESSOR DUMBLEDORE . . . YOU MEANT A GREAT DEAL TO HIM."
>
> Professor McGonagall to Harry Potter, *Harry Potter and the Half-Blood Prince*

NO ONE'S PERFECT

During the Triwizard Tournament in *Harry Potter and the Goblet of Fire*, "Dumbledore feels responsible for all the children, though especially Harry," says Michael Gambon. "And then evil comes into the castle, [and] he can't deal with it initially." Gambon thinks that Harry now sees Dumbledore as a man who isn't perfect. "He doesn't know everything, and that must be quite a shock for him. He has to learn a new way of dealing with things."

EQUAL TO THE TASK

Harry and Dumbledore's relationship goes beyond headmaster and student in *Harry Potter and the Half-Blood Prince* when they pursue a Horcrux hidden by Voldemort in a dangerous crystal cave. To retrieve the Horcrux, Dumbledore must drink a foul potion from a liquid-filled basin and must trust Harry's strength to help him, though he begs for relief. "Right in front of Dumbledore, Harry's turning into a young man," says Gambon. "It turns into a friendship, a closeness."

SOLDIERING ON

Daniel Radcliffe believes the relationship between Harry and Dumbledore started off like father and son, "which worked quite nicely. But as it becomes more about stopping Voldemort, Harry becomes a foot soldier under orders in Dumbledore's Army." When Dumbledore dies, in *Harry Potter and the Half-Blood Prince*, "Now Harry's the one who has to make the plans," Radcliffe says. "I think it focuses him even more toward finding Voldemort."

Dumbledore feels the need to avoid Harry in *Harry Potter and the Order of the Phoenix*. "He thinks Voldemort might be using Harry as a way of seeing him through what Harry's seeing," says Daniel Radcliffe. "Sadly, Dumbledore is ignoring Harry at a time when Harry actually needs him the most."

MINERVA McGONAGALL

Professor Minerva McGonagall, played by actress Dame Maggie Smith, is the Transfiguration professor, Head of Gryffindor house, and a stalwart supporter of Harry Potter.

SOFT SPOT

Dame Maggie describes her character as both stern and a softy, especially when it comes to Harry, Ron, and Hermione. "She's the one who keeps them in order. She's fairly fierce because she has to keep some discipline throughout the school, but cares very much about them, obviously. She's very, very fond of Harry. I think you can tell that."

WIZARD'S WALTZ

Fourth-year and above students dance at the Yule Ball, in *Harry Potter and the Goblet of Fire*, and were given dancing lessons by Professor McGonagall, who selects Ron Weasley to demonstrate the waltz. Rupert Grint (Ron) found dancing with Dame Maggie "a memorable moment." Dame Maggie recalls the scene as "strenuous! Poor Ron! I mean, I've got two left feet, too, so we both looked pretty silly!"

> "WHY IS IT WHEN SOMETHING HAPPENS IT IS ALWAYS YOU THREE?"
>
> Professor Minerva McGonagall,
> *Harry Potter and the Half-Blood Prince*

RUBEUS HAGRID

Actor Robbie Coltrane plays Rubeus Hagrid, Keeper of Keys and Grounds at Hogwarts and a friend to every creature, whether nice or dangerous. He's beloved by most of the Hogwarts students. As Harry tells him, "There's no Hogwarts without you, Hagrid."

BEST INTERESTS AT HEART

"Hagrid doesn't have an agenda," says Coltrane. "His only interest is looking after Harry. It's Hagrid who delivered him that night, and he feels a very, very strong protective love for the wee fellow. It was Hagrid who told Harry that he was a wizard. He was the guy who said, Look, you're the special one. You're the one who beat You-Know-Who. And you've got to understand that you have a very important place in the history of magic. He's very serious."

Robbie Coltrane feels it's important that Hagrid is not an authority figure. "He doesn't live in the castle, so he's not actually part of the establishment. But, of course, he knows what's going on, so he's a very good ally to have."

> "FAME'S A FICKLE FRIEND, HARRY."
>
> Professor Lockhart,
> *Harry Potter and the Chamber of Secrets*

Professor Pomona Sprout, played by Miriam Margolyes, teaches Herbology. In *Harry Potter and the Chamber of Secrets*, her first lesson with Harry and his classmates is repotting Mandrakes. Sprout will later use these for a Mandrake Restorative Draught to revive Hermione Granger and other students who were Petrified during encounters with the Basilisk.

FILIUS FLITWICK ✦ GILDEROY LOCKHART

Charms professor Filius Flitwick is played by Warwick Davis who, in *Harry Potter and the Sorcerer's Stone*, imagined the elderly professor was "understanding, fun, and in with the pupils. The kind of teacher I would have liked to have had at school."

> "PROFESSOR FLITWICK, YOU'VE KNOWN ME FOR FIVE YEARS."
>
> "NO EXCEPTIONS . . . POTTER."
>
> Harry Potter and Professor Flitwick,
> *Harry Potter and the Half-Blood Prince*

Harry meets Professor Gilderoy Lockhart, his second-year Defense Against the Dark Arts professor, when Lockhart pulls Harry into a photo shoot for the *Daily Prophet*. "It's a burden to be Gilderoy Lockhart, but it has to be done," says actor Kenneth Branagh. "[Lockhart] loves publicity. [He] loves people asking for his autograph and feels as though— it may not be mutual—that he's found a soul mate in Harry Potter."

SYBILL TRELAWNEY

Professor Sybill Trelawney, played by Emma Thompson, teaches Divination, the art of using various methods to see the future. The bespectacled seer determined Harry's life, in a way, by uttering a prophecy heralding a newborn with the ability to overthrow the Dark Lord, who Voldemort interpreted as Harry Potter.

> "THE ONE WITH THE POWER TO VANQUISH THE DARK LORD APPROACHES . . ."
>
> Professor Trelawney, *Harry Potter and the Prisoner of Azkaban*

HORACE SLUGHORN

Horace Slughorn is a former Potions professor whom Dumbledore persuades to return to Hogwarts in *Harry Potter and the Half-Blood Prince*. Slughorn possesses a memory that indicates how to destroy Voldemort, and Harry finds a way to retrieve it.

> "ANY FRIEND OF HARRY'S IS A FRIEND OF MINE."
>
> Professor Slughorn, *Harry Potter and the Half-Blood Prince*

Harry wins a vial of Felix Felicis—Liquid Luck—in Slughorn's class that helps him recover the needed memory.

REMUS LUPIN

Professor Remus Lupin, played by David Thewlis, is the Defense Against the Dark Arts professor in *Harry Potter and the Prisoner of Azkaban*. Lupin is one of the last surviving links to Harry's parents.

FEEDBACK

Harry meets Professor Lupin on the Hogwarts Express, where he saves him from an attack by one of the foulest creatures on earth—a Dementor. Dementors "feed on every good feeling, every happy memory," Lupin explains later, "until a person is left with nothing but his worst experiences." Lupin always keeps an antidote to Dementors in his pocket: chocolate.

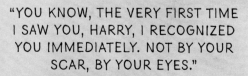

"YOU KNOW, THE VERY FIRST TIME I SAW YOU, HARRY, I RECOGNIZED YOU IMMEDIATELY. NOT BY YOUR SCAR, BY YOUR EYES."

Professor Remus Lupin,
Harry Potter and the Prisoner of Azkaban

AVUNCULAR

Thewlis believes the foundation of Harry and Lupin's relationship is his connection to James and Lily Potter. "Lupin explains what Harry's parents were like," says Thewlis. "He's one of the only people who can actually tell Harry about them firsthand. He's a great comfort to Harry, which was part of the appeal of the character to me."

MAJOR KEY

Daniel Radcliffe calls Remus Lupin instrumental to the films.
"Through him, Harry learns a lot about his mom and dad," he says,
which answers many questions Harry holds about his past. Radcliffe
and Thewlis enjoyed filming the scenes between these characters.
"The key emotional scenes [in *Prisoner of Azkaban*] make up the heart
of the film," Radcliffe explains. "And they seem to me to be between
Harry and Lupin almost every time."

Lupin protects Harry
during a class exercise
where a Boggart
changes into a student's
worst fear. Later, Lupin
teaches him how to cast
the Patronus Charm
against Dementors.

SUCCESS HAS MANY FATHERS

Remus Lupin becomes less of an uncle and more of a father
figure to Harry in *Harry Potter and the Deathly Hallows – Parts 1
and 2*. "Sirius and Dumbledore are gone," says Thewlis, "and
Harry's running out of protectors." Lupin gives his life at the
Battle of Hogwarts. "So, it seems, unfortunately, that it's the kiss
of death to be his protector," he adds dryly.

Voldemort

Lord Voldemort, the most powerful Dark wizard in his time, was threatened by a prophecy about a boy who would be able to defeat him. The Dark Lord determines this is the infant Harry Potter and casts the Killing Curse at him. Protected by his mother's love, the curse rebounds off Harry, and Voldemort becomes an ethereal specter.

✦ ✦ ✦

In *Harry Potter and the Order of the Phoenix*, Voldemort possesses Harry physically after a battle with Dumbledore in the Ministry of Magic. It is the thoughts of the friends and family who love him that save Harry and allow him to expel the Dark Lord.

"YOU'RE THE WEAK ONE. AND YOU'LL NEVER KNOW LOVE OR FRIENDSHIP. AND I FEEL SORRY FOR YOU."

Harry Potter, *Harry Potter and the Order of the Phoenix*

A CAPTIVE AUDIENCE

Voldemort, played by Ralph Fiennes, becomes corporeal in *Harry Potter and the Goblet of Fire* and tortures Harry. "I felt bad because Daniel had to express pain and agony and fear while I did a *lot* of talking," says Fiennes. Fiennes found it a challenge to be "really horrible" to Harry "because everyone loves him!"

·⟩⟩⟩ · ⟩⟩⟩ · ⟩⟩⟩ ·⟩⟩⟩ ·⟩⟩⟩ · ⟩⟩⟩ · ⟩⟩⟩ ·⟩⟩⟩

UNCONDITIONAL

"Harry realizes that Voldemort may have the numbers," says Daniel Radcliffe, "but ultimately, he will never have what Harry has, which is true and unconditional loyalty." Radcliffe believes that Voldemort's followers only follow him because they would be tortured or killed if they left. "Whereas, the people who surround Harry and the people Harry looks up to—whatever happens, they will stand by each other."

After Harry comes to Hogwarts, Voldemort attempts to eliminate him through Quirinus Quirrell, a Defense Against the Dark Arts professor, in *Harry Potter and the Sorcerer's Stone*, and a memory of himself in a magical diary, in *Harry Potter and the Chamber of Secrets*.

DOLORES UMBRIDGE

Dolores Umbridge comes from her job as Senior Undersecretary at the Ministry of Magic to take the post of Defense Against the Dark Arts professor in *Harry Potter and the Order of the Phoenix*. Umbridge, played by Imelda Staunton, teaches a Ministry-approved lesson plan that does not allow her students to practice defensive spells.

A FIRM HAND

Umbridge gives Harry Potter detention after he talks about Voldemort returning, making him write "I must not tell lies" using a pen she provides. The pen uses the writer's blood, and the words scar the back of Harry's hand. "I felt terrible after that scene," says Staunton. "I thought it was horrible. And it's alarming that people think punishment is a way of teaching someone, and she believes that is true."

During her tenure, Umbridge organizes the Inquisitorial Squad, a group of mostly Slytherin students who are tasked with catching Dumbledore's Army.

CLASS WARFARE

The very thing Umbridge is trying to prevent impels the students to create Dumbledore's Army. "Harry ends up absolutely loving teaching the kids," says Daniel Radcliffe. "Harry is such a lonely person; even when he's in a crowded room, he's completely alone. But in the class when he's teaching, he doesn't have to worry about his own problems. He only has to worry about what they're doing. That's him at his most comfortable, I think."

RETURN OF THE PINK

Umbridge returns in *Harry Potter and the Deathly Hallows – Part 1* as the Head of the Ministry's Muggle-Born Registration Commission. "To her, it's necessary to weed out those wizards who aren't pure-bloods," Staunton explains. "But I think this is just her, once again, making the most of what really little power she has."

LUCIUS AND NARCISSA MALFOY

Lucius and Narcissa are the parents of Harry's school nemesis, Draco Malfoy, and devoted followers of Voldemort.

DEATH EATERS

Jason Isaacs portrays Lucius Malfoy. "Lucius is a thoroughly unpleasant man," says Isaacs. "He believes in pure blood and is about as bigoted as you can get." In *Harry Potter and the Chamber of Secrets*, Lucius passes the Dark artifact of Tom Riddle's diary to Ginny Weasley, who, possessed, reopens the Chamber of Secrets.

·⟩⟩⟩ · ⟩⟩⟩ · ⟩⟩⟩ · ⟩⟩⟩ · ⟩⟩⟩ · ⟩⟩⟩ · ⟩⟩⟩ · ⟩⟩⟩

Helen McCrory plays Draco's mother, Narcissa, whose belief in Voldemort's cause is tested when he gives her son a dangerous task to fulfill. Later, Narcissa lies to Voldemort that he has killed Harry when he has not, in *Harry Potter and the Deathly Hallows – Part 2*. "You have to understand what a woman does to keep her child alive. And what that is, is anything," said McCrory. "So, she's a baddie but a good mother."

and the Deathly Hallows – Part 1

BELLATRIX LESTRANGE

Bellatrix Lestrange is Narcissa Malfoy's sister and perhaps the most rabid follower of Voldemort. Bellatrix is played by Helena Bonham Carter, who admits, "I probably made her a bit more unhinged than she was meant to be. But you can't really phone Bellatrix in."

AVADA KEDAVRA

Bellatrix joins other Death Eaters at the Ministry's Department of Mysteries, in *Harry Potter and the Order of the Phoenix*, to acquire the prophecy concerning Harry and Voldemort. There, they battle members of Dumbledore's Army. Taking the opportunity, Bellatrix casts the Killing Curse at Sirius Black, her own cousin and Harry's godfather.

During the First Wizarding War, Bellatrix cast the Cruciatus Curse at Neville Longbottom's parents.

CASTING DOUBT

"When Bellatrix kills Sirius," says Daniel Radcliffe, "she becomes the focus of Harry's hate." Harry casts the Cruciatus Curse at her but doesn't succeed. "In his anger, he sees a side of himself that will absolutely kill someone," says Daniel Radcliffe. "That's a scary moment of self-realization. If he gives in to these thoughts of revenge, then he's in real danger of becoming like Voldemort."

FRIEND OR FOE?

✶⊹ DOBBY ⊹✶

Dobby is a house-elf with big eyes, big ears, and big intentions to keep Harry safe, but his "help" often backfires, with Harry getting in trouble, or worse. A house-elf is bound to serve one wizarding family no matter what, and Dobby's master is a cruel one.

BEST INTENTIONS

Dobby has learned that harm will come to Harry if he returns to Hogwarts, so the house-elf does what he can to prevent Harry's return throughout *Harry Potter and the Chamber of Secrets*. He hides mail from Harry's friends, drops a cake on an important client of Harry's uncle's, seals the entrance to Platform Nine and Three-Quarters, and even causes a Bludger to attack Harry in a game of Quidditch.

Harry learns what family Dobby serves—the Malfoys—and finds a way to release the house-elf from his service. When Dobby asks how he can repay Harry for releasing him, he asks Dobby to promise never to save his life again.

ALONE TOGETHER

Dobby was the first entirely digital character in the Harry Potter films, so when Harry interacted with the house-elf, "Daniel wouldn't have anyone in the room to act with," says *Chamber of Secrets* director Chris Columbus. "He was basically acting with a tennis ball on a stick. But Dan was so focused, he made you believe Dobby was there."

"NOT TO BE RUDE OR ANYTHING, BUT THIS ISN'T A GREAT TIME FOR ME TO HAVE A HOUSE-ELF IN MY BEDROOM."

Harry Potter, *Harry Potter and the Chamber of Secrets*

FRIEND!

"DOBBY IS HAPPY TO BE WITH HIS FRIEND, HARRY POTTER."

Dobby, *Harry Potter and the Deathly Hallows – Part 1*

GOOD TROUBLE

Dobby returns in *Harry Potter and the Deathly Hallows – Part 1* to save Harry and his friends, this time successfully. At Malfoy Manor, Lucius Malfoy, played by Jason Isaacs, presses the Death Eater mark on his arm to summon Voldemort, "but just before it all works out," says Isaacs, "that nasty little pointy-eared git Dobby reappears and whisks my victory away. I should have dealt with that elf when I had the chance!"

A FRIEND'S LOVE

Sadly, Dobby is killed by Bellatrix Lestrange. "Dobby's death enforces Harry's commitment to defeat the Dark Lord, no matter what," says director David Yates. Harry, Ron, and Hermione dig Dobby's grave themselves, without magic. Actor Daniel Radcliffe thought that was fitting and right. "Harry wants to invest as much love in Dobby's burial as Dobby showed him throughout his life," he explains.

SIRIUS BLACK

"Notorious mass murderer" Sirius Black is believed to have betrayed James and Lily Potter to Voldemort and murdered twelve Muggles and the wizard Peter Pettigrew. Now, Sirius has escaped from Azkaban prison, and word is out he's looking for Harry Potter.

> "I WOULD HAVE DIED RATHER THAN BETRAY MY FRIENDS!"
>
> Sirius Black,
> *Harry Potter
> and the Prisoner
> of Azkaban*

BETRAYED BY A FRIEND

In *Harry Potter and the Prisoner of Azkaban*, Harry learns that Sirius is innocent of wrongdoing. "Everybody thinks I'm this dark figure," says actor Gary Oldman (Sirius Black). "So, right up to the last minute, you must think I'm after Harry." But it's not Harry he wants. "It's the rat I'm after." "The rat" is the Animagus Peter Pettigrew, transformed as Ron's rat, Scabbers.

FOE!

THE BEST OF FRIENDS

Sirius Black was at Hogwarts with James Potter and Remus Lupin, and "we were the best of friends," says Oldman. "So much that when Harry is born, James and Lily make me the godfather to Harry. When you pick someone as a godparent, you don't do that lightly."

Sirius tries to break into the Gryffindor common room in his Animagus form of a large dog. He slashes the portrait of the Fat Lady, who guards the entrance, but can't get inside.

> ## "KEEP YOUR FRIENDS CLOSE, HARRY."
>
> Sirius Black, *Harry Potter and the Goblet of Fire*

FOLLOWING ORDERS

Sirius accompanies Harry to King's Cross in *Harry Potter and the Order of the Phoenix*. While there, Sirius presents Harry with a photograph of the original Order. "I think this is his way of saying, 'You're the heir to the new Order,'" says Oldman.

NOT SO SURE

While at 12 Grimmauld Place, the headquarters of the Order of the Phoenix, Harry wonders to Sirius if he is turning into a bad person. "Ever since the Sorting Hat said, 'You should be in Slytherin,' Harry worries about his potential for evil, made even stronger because of his connection to Voldemort," says Daniel Radcliffe. "And then Sirius says one of my favorite lines: 'You are not a bad person. You're a very good person who bad things have happened to.' It absolutely sums up Harry's situation."

Harry's scream of pain when Sirius Black dies was slowed down and muted, so that the audience could process the death.

LOST IN THE PAST

During a wand battle between Death Eaters and the Order of the Phoenix in the Ministry of Magic, Harry and Sirius duel with Lucius Malfoy. When Harry manages to disarm Malfoy, Sirius calls out, "Nice one, James." "I'm back fourteen years, in the old days," says Oldman, "and living a friendship through Harry, who's so like James."

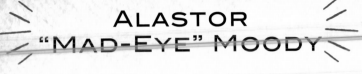

ALASTOR "MAD-EYE" MOODY

Alastor "Mad-Eye" Moody is invited by Albus Dumbledore to teach Defense Against the Dark Arts in *Harry Potter and the Goblet of Fire*. Moody is a notorious Dark wizard catcher and a member of the Order of the Phoenix, founded by Dumbledore to fight against Voldemort and his Death Eaters.

Moody keeps a Foe-Glass in his office, as it "lets me keep an eye on my enemies," he tells Harry. The "foe" in Foe-Glass turns out to be true during Harry's fourth year.

FOE!

INSIDE JOB

"Moody is called in because there are evil times looming," explains actor Brendan Gleeson, "and he's here to protect Harry." But before Moody can arrive, he is kidnapped by the Death Eater Barty Crouch Jr., who drinks Polyjuice Potion to disguise himself as the ex-Auror. "So," Gleeson continues, "what you see is not what you get with Moody."

ON HIS SIDE

Members of the Order, including the real Moody, transport Harry to their headquarters in *Harry Potter and the Order of the Phoenix*. "Moody is paranoid according to other people, but he can feel the danger that's around," says Gleeson. "I think he feels it in the same way Harry does, making him a kindred spirit. As Harry's been maligned as telling lies, Mad-Eye has had the same kind of experience."

❖❖❖❖❖❖❖❖❖❖❖❖❖❖

DRIVE TO DISTRACT

Moody assembles six Polyjuice-transformed decoys of Harry to distract the Death Eaters' attention as he leaves Little Whinging in *Harry Potter and the Deathly Hallows – Part 1*. During the deception, Moody is killed, and Harry loses another father figure, according to Gleeson. "I've always felt that Mad-Eye was quite a strong one, even when he was invaded by somebody else," he explains. "But nevertheless, his heart was always in the right place."

DRACO MALFOY

Draco Malfoy, played by Tom Felton, becomes a rival and bully to Harry Potter almost immediately upon their acquaintance as children. Raised in a wealthy—and bigoted—wizard family, he is narrow-minded and resentful of Harry's celebrity.

> "YOU'LL SOON FIND THAT SOME WIZARDING FAMILIES ARE BETTER THAN OTHERS, POTTER. YOU DON'T WANT TO GO MAKING FRIENDS WITH THE WRONG SORT. I CAN HELP YOU THERE."
>
> "I THINK I CAN TELL WHO THE WRONG SORT ARE FOR MYSELF, THANKS."
>
> Draco Malfoy and Harry Potter, *Harry Potter and the Sorcerer's Stone*

LIKE FATHER

Draco Malfoy doesn't have the healthiest relationship with his father. "It was my intention that if you saw how much of a bully Lucius was," says Jason Isaacs, "you would begin to understand the behavior that Draco is aping at school."

·)))·)))·)))·)))·)))·)))·)))·)))

WAIT FOR IT

Draco and Harry have a more consequential duel in *Harry Potter and the Half-Blood Prince*, in a boys' bathroom. "Dan and I have been waiting years to kill each other," says Felton. "Our relationship was almost lighthearted at first. There was never really any physical violence, and it was always mainly a bit of mouth. Whereas this time, it's certainly got deeper, to say the least."

In *Harry Potter and the Chamber of Secrets*, Draco and Harry face off in a Dueling Club wand battle. Draco cheats: He jumps the count of three and throws a spell he isn't supposed to, which hurls Harry backward.

When Lucius Malfoy is imprisoned in Azkaban, in *Harry Potter and the Half-Blood Prince*, Draco begins to show a more vulnerable side. "[Draco's] really a victim of circumstance more than anything," says Felton. "He's a normal kid surrounded by some of the worst influences children could be around—some pretty awful parents, Lucius and Narcissa, and Bellatrix. Maybe we misread this guy."

REDEEMING FEATURES

When asked to confirm if it is Harry disguised by a Stinging Jinx, in *Harry Potter and the Deathly Hallows – Part 1*, Draco replies he can't be sure. "He doesn't even realize himself what he's doing," says Felton. "He just knows deep down he doesn't want to kill Harry. As hard as he would want to be like his dad, he can't."

SEVERUS SNAPE

Is Potions professor Severus Snape Harry's foe or friend? That question was constantly raised throughout the eight Harry Potter films and only answered at the end. Actor Alan Rickman played Snape with an enigmatic air of loathing Harry, while at the same time protecting and even defending him.

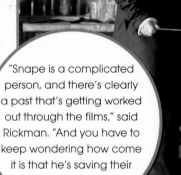

> "Snape is a complicated person, and there's clearly a past that's getting worked out through the films," said Rickman. "And you have to keep wondering how come it is that he's saving their lives all the time."

> ## "SNAPE WAS TRYING TO SAVE ME?"
> Harry Potter, *Harry Potter and the Sorcerer's Stone*

TOO TRUE

From the beginning, Severus Snape is mean to Harry, who does not understand why. "Alan Rickman was so fantastic as Severus Snape, I was freaked," says Daniel Radcliffe. "I was constantly having to remind myself: 'It's only a film, it's only a film, it's only a film . . . nothing's real,' but it was terrifying."

BAD INSTINCTS

Daniel Radcliffe believes that Harry is instinctual in his judgment of people and was immediately suspect of Snape. "When he meets someone, it'll be pretty instant whether he likes them or not," he explains. "So, it's an important lesson for Harry that you have to give someone a chance before you actually know who they are."

FOE!

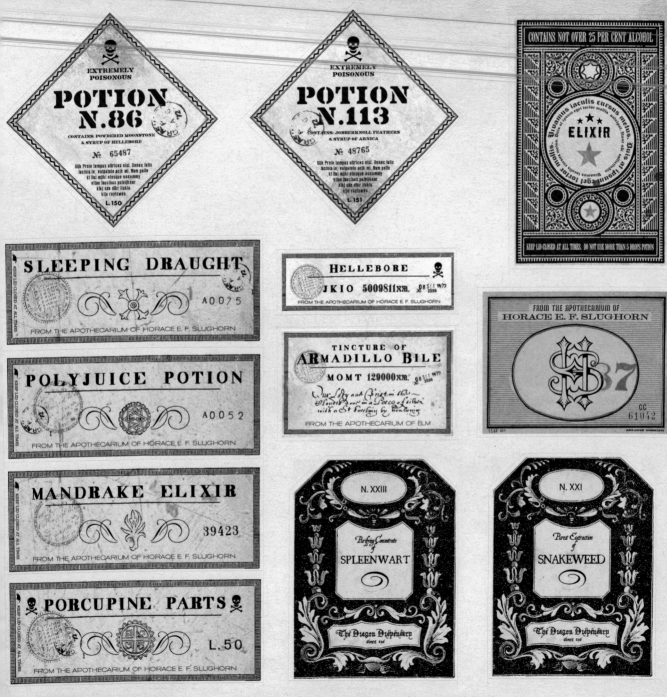

EXTREMELY
POISONOUS

POTION
N.86

CONTAINS: POWDERED MOONSTONE
& SYRUP OF HELLEBORE

№ 65487

Sijk Proin tempus ultrices nisl. Donec felis
lacinia in, vulputate acjk mi. Nam pelle
ki thui mjki ntesque nonummy
vitae faucibus pulvikear
kikj sde dikr ilukiu
kiju raytnwen

L. 150

EXTREMELY
POISONOUS

POTION
N.113

CONTAINS: JOBBERKNOLL FEATHERS
& SYRUP OF ARNICA

№ 48765

Sijk Proin tempus ultrices nisl. Donec felis
lacinia in, vulputate acjk mi. Nam pelle
ki thui mjki ntesque nonummy
vitae faucibus pulvikear
kikj sde dikr ilukiu
kiju raytnwen

L. 151

CONTAINS NOT OVER 25 PER CENT ALCOHOL

ELIXIR

Vivamus iaculis cursus metus. Duis
Duis ut ipsum eget tortor mollis. Duis ut ipsum eget tortor mollis

KEEP LID CLOSED AT ALL TIMES. DO NOT USE MORE THAN 5 DROPS POTION

SLEEPING DRAUGHT

KEEP LID CLOSED AT ALL TIMES

A 0075

FROM THE APOTHECARIUM OF HORACE E. F. SLUGHORN

POLYJUICE POTION

KEEP LID CLOSED AT ALL TIMES

A 0052

FROM THE APOTHECARIUM OF HORACE E. F. SLUGHORN

MANDRAKE ELIXIR

KEEP LID CLOSED AT ALL TIMES

39423

FROM THE APOTHECARIUM OF HORACE E. F. SLUGHORN

☠ PORCUPINE PARTS ☠

KEEP LID CLOSED AT ALL TIMES

L. 50

FROM THE APOTHECARIUM OF HORACE E. F. SLUGHORN

HELLEBORE ☠

JKIO 5009811nm.

08 SEP 1877
2599

FROM THE APOTHECARIUM OF HORACE E. F. SLUGHORN

TINCTURE OF
ARMADILLO BILE

MOMT 129000nm.

08 SEP 1877
2599

FROM THE APOTHECARIUM OF ELM

FROM THE APOTHECARIUM OF
HORACE E. F. SLUGHORN

87

CC
61042

N. XXIII

Purifying Concentrate
of
SPLEENWART

The Dragon Dispensary
since 156

N. XXI

Purest Extraction
of
SNAKEWEED

The Dragon Dispensary
since 156

FRIEND!

KICK BACK

In *Harry Potter and the Order of the Phoenix*, Snape tries to teach Harry how to prevent Voldemort from gaining access to his thoughts. When Harry uses this magic against Snape, he views a memory that shows his father, James, bullying Snape when they were students. "Harry sees my dad was to Snape what Draco Malfoy is to me," says Radcliffe. "And if you really hated someone, what you would hate even more was learning that the hatred they felt toward you actually had some justification."

After Harry, Hermione, and Ron exit the Whomping Willow in *Harry Potter and the Prisoner of Azkaban,* Snape does his best to protect them when Remus Lupin changes into a werewolf.

SECRET KEEPER

"It was such a wonderful mystery," says Daniel Radcliffe, "wondering if this guy is good or bad— that had people going for years. He's a character that stepped directly out of people's imaginations. Exactly as you would picture Snape, there was Alan Rickman."

INSIGHT EDITIONS

PO Box 3088
San Rafael, CA 94912
www.insighteditions.com

f Find us on Facebook: www.facebook.com/InsightEditions
🐦 Follow us on Twitter: @insighteditions

Library of Congress Cataloging-in-Publication Data available.

ISBN: 978-1-64722-435-6

Publisher: Raoul Goff
VP of Licensing and Partnerships: Vanessa Lopez
VP of Creative: Chrissy Kwasnik
VP of Manufacturing: Alix Nicholaeff
Editorial Director: Vicki Jaeger
Designer: Leah Lauer
Associate Editor: Anna Wostenberg
Senior Production Editor: Elaine Ou
Senior Production Manager: Greg Steffen
Senior Production Manager, Subsidiary Rights: Lina s Palma

Insight Editions, in association with Roots of Peace, will plant two trees for each tree used in the manufacturing of this book. Roots of Peace is an internationally renowned humanitarian organization dedicated to eradicating land mines worldwide and converting war-torn lands into productive farms and wildlife habitats. Roots of Peace will plant two million fruit and nut trees in Afghanistan and provide farmers there with the skills and support necessary for sustainable land use.

Manufactured in China by Insight Editions

10 9 8 7 6 5 4 3 2 1